DIGGING UP BONES!
FAMOUS ARCHAEOLOGY DISCOVERIES ARCHAEOLOGY FOR KIDS CHILDREN'S ARCHAEOLOGY BOOKS

pfiffikus
EDUCATIONAL BOOKS FOR CHILDREN K-12

All Rights reserved. No part of this book may be reproduced or used in any way or form or by any means whether electronic or mechanical, this means that you cannot record or photocopy any material ideas or tips that are provided in this book

Copyright 2016

Archaeology is a branch of science that studies prehistoric and historic people. Archeologists dig up artifacts, monuments, inscriptions and other remains to use as subjects of their studies. Here are some of the greatest archaeological discoveries in history.

...SI ELVOMO SOME...
...VENDER O FAR VEND...
...OCO DELLA CIT...
...ARCHE NE PER L...
...SANTI APOSTOLI...
...PRECIOV...

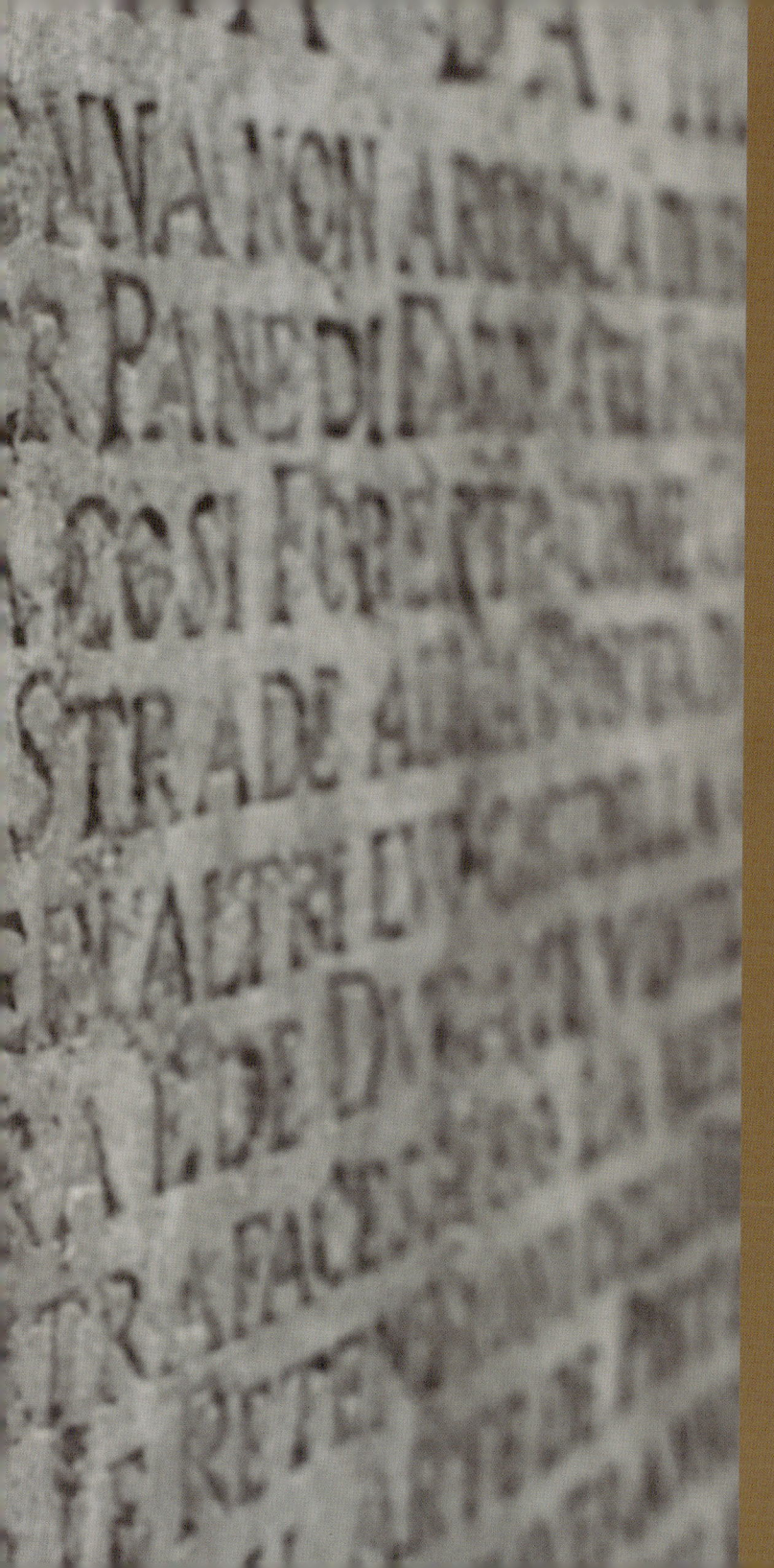

Rosetta Stone

Discovered in 1799 by a French expedition, the Rosetta Stone is an upright slab stone used as building material in ancient Egypt.

It had an inscription of a decree issued in Memphis, Egypt in behalf of King Ptolemy V.

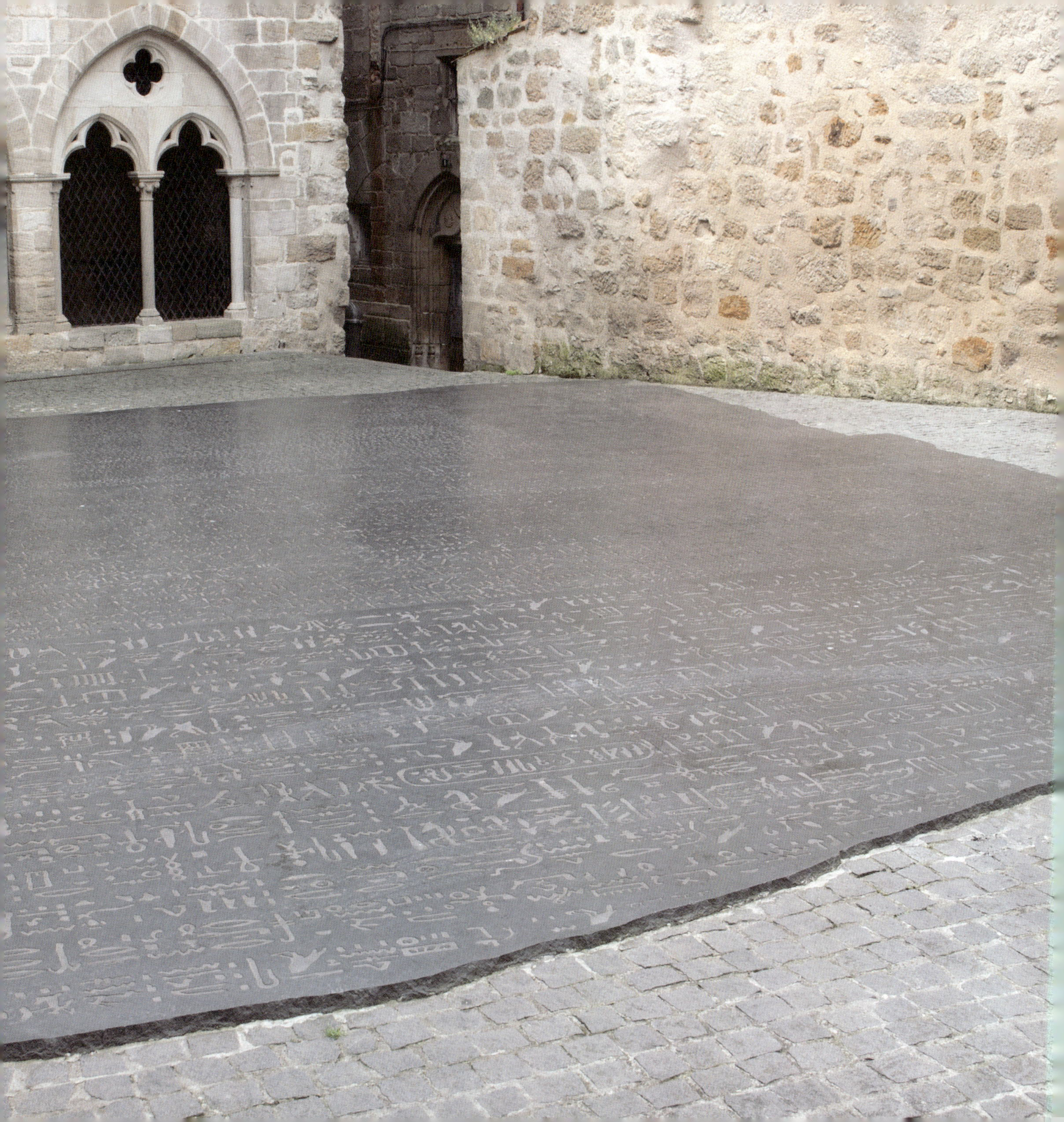

The decree appeared in the form of three scripts; the upper text showed hieroglyphs of the ancient Egyptian, the middle text showed the demotic script, and its lowest script was of the ancient Greek.

The Rosetta stone led to a better understanding of the Egyptian hieroglyphs.

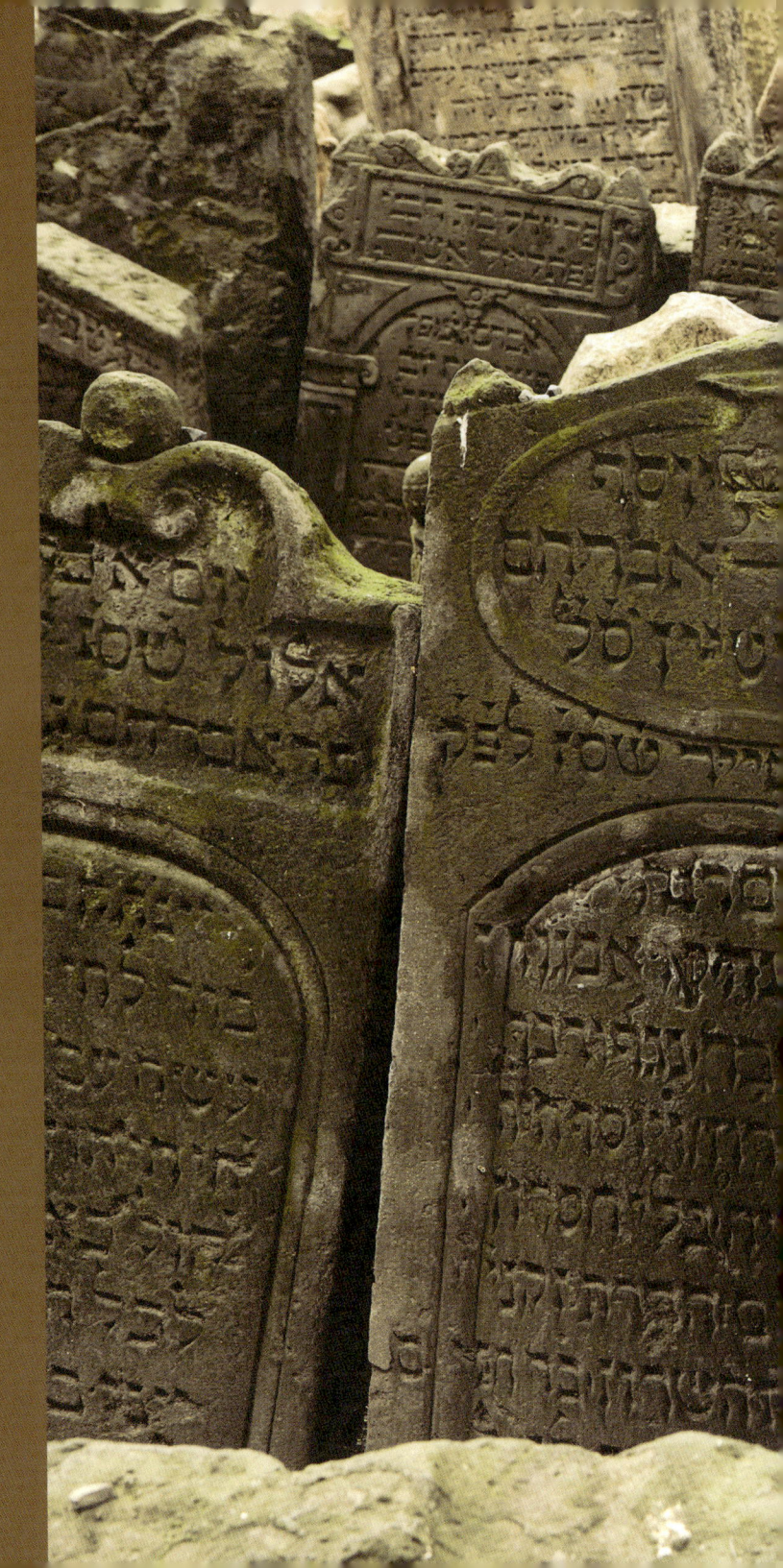

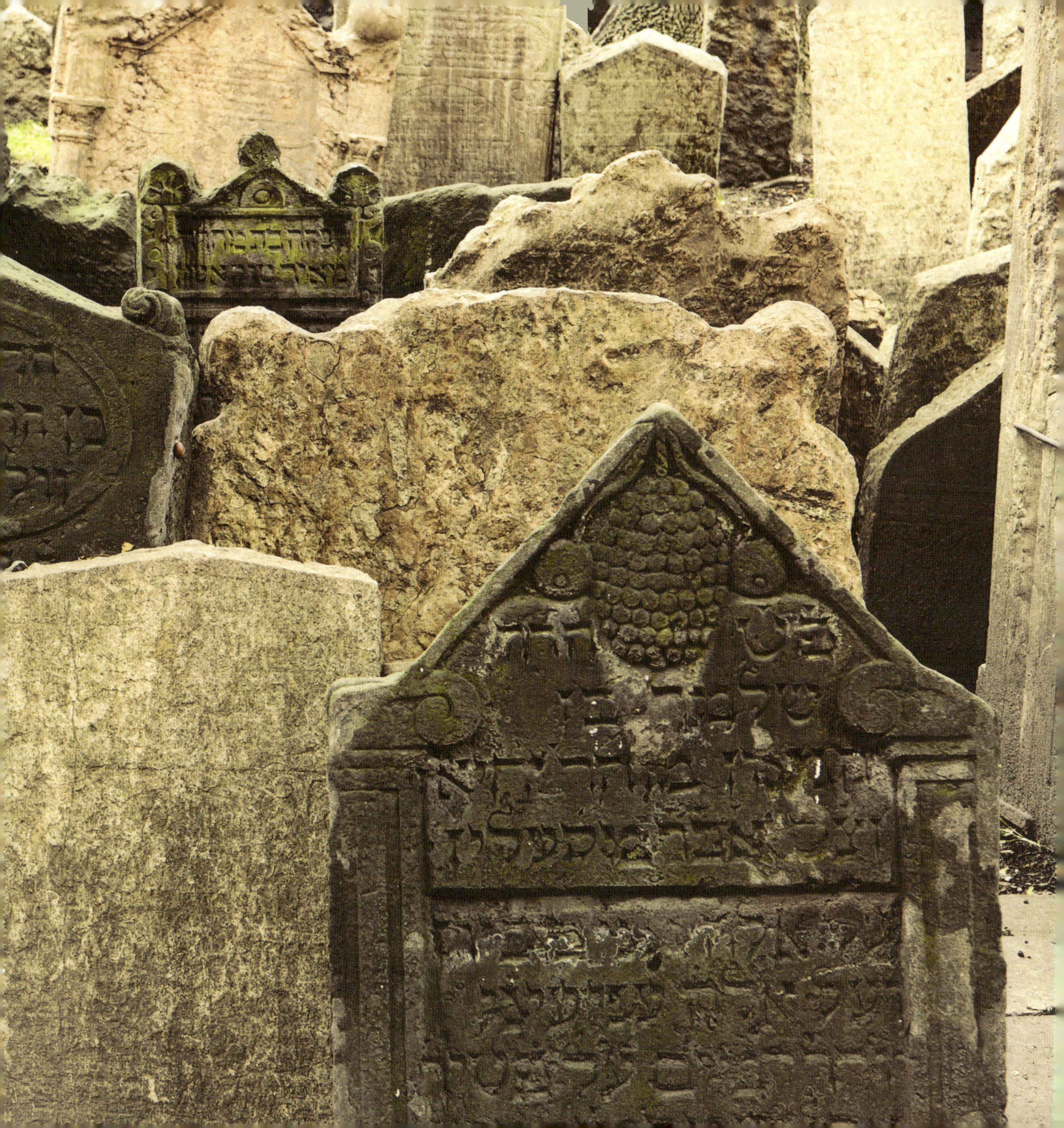

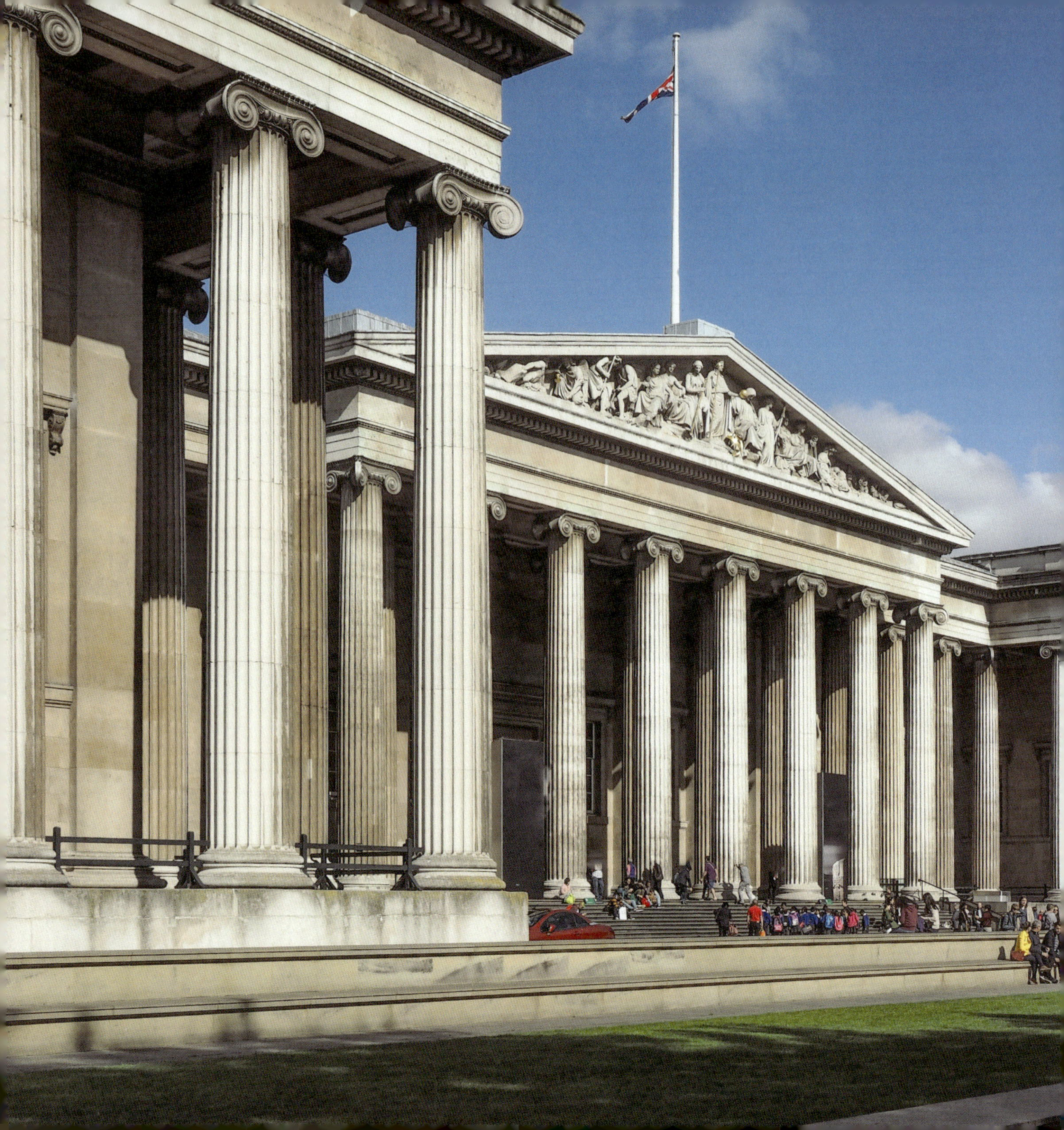

The Rosetta Stone was seized by the British on 1801, and a year later, it was moved to the British Museum, where it sits until today.

Dead Sea Scrolls

The Dead Sea Scrolls are a collection of around 981 biblical manuscripts that were found inside the eleven caves of Khirbet Qumran in the West Bank.

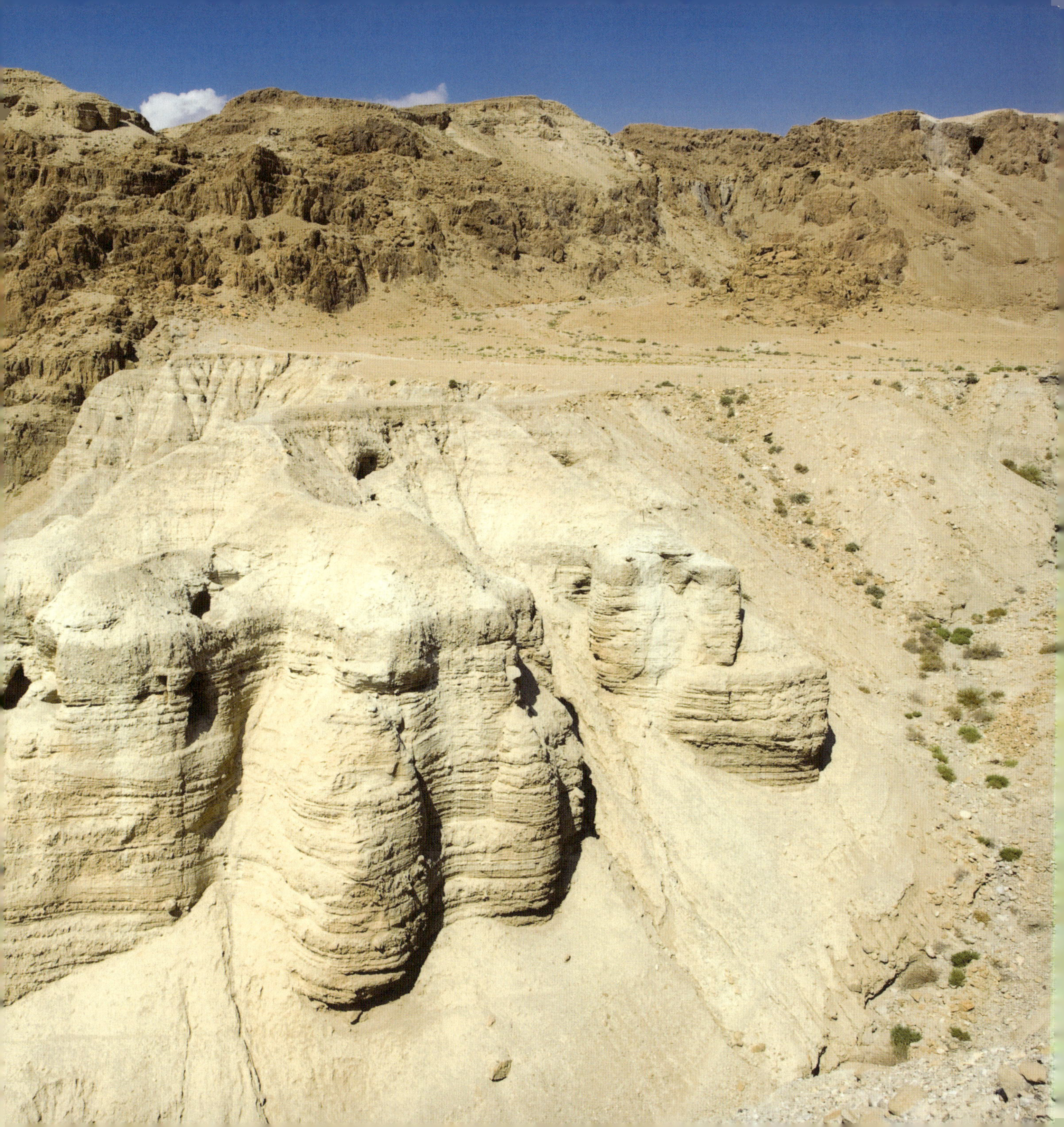

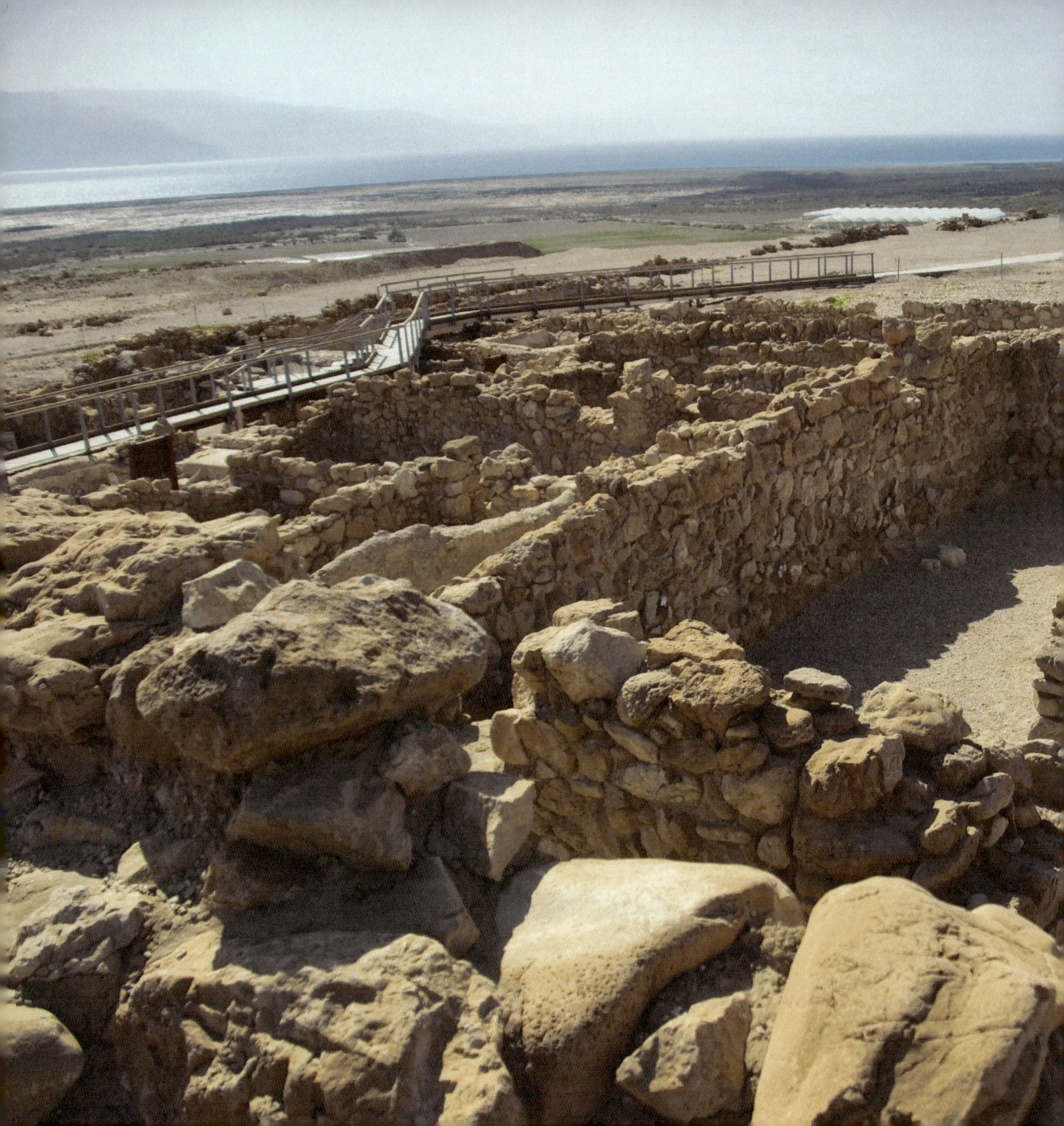

These caves are located just 1.2 miles inland off the Dead Sea's northwest shore. The scrolls were written in Hebrew Bible canon, together with extra-biblical and deuterocanonical manuscripts.

These scrolls are preserved evidence showing the diversity of the religious thought during the late Second Temple Judaism.

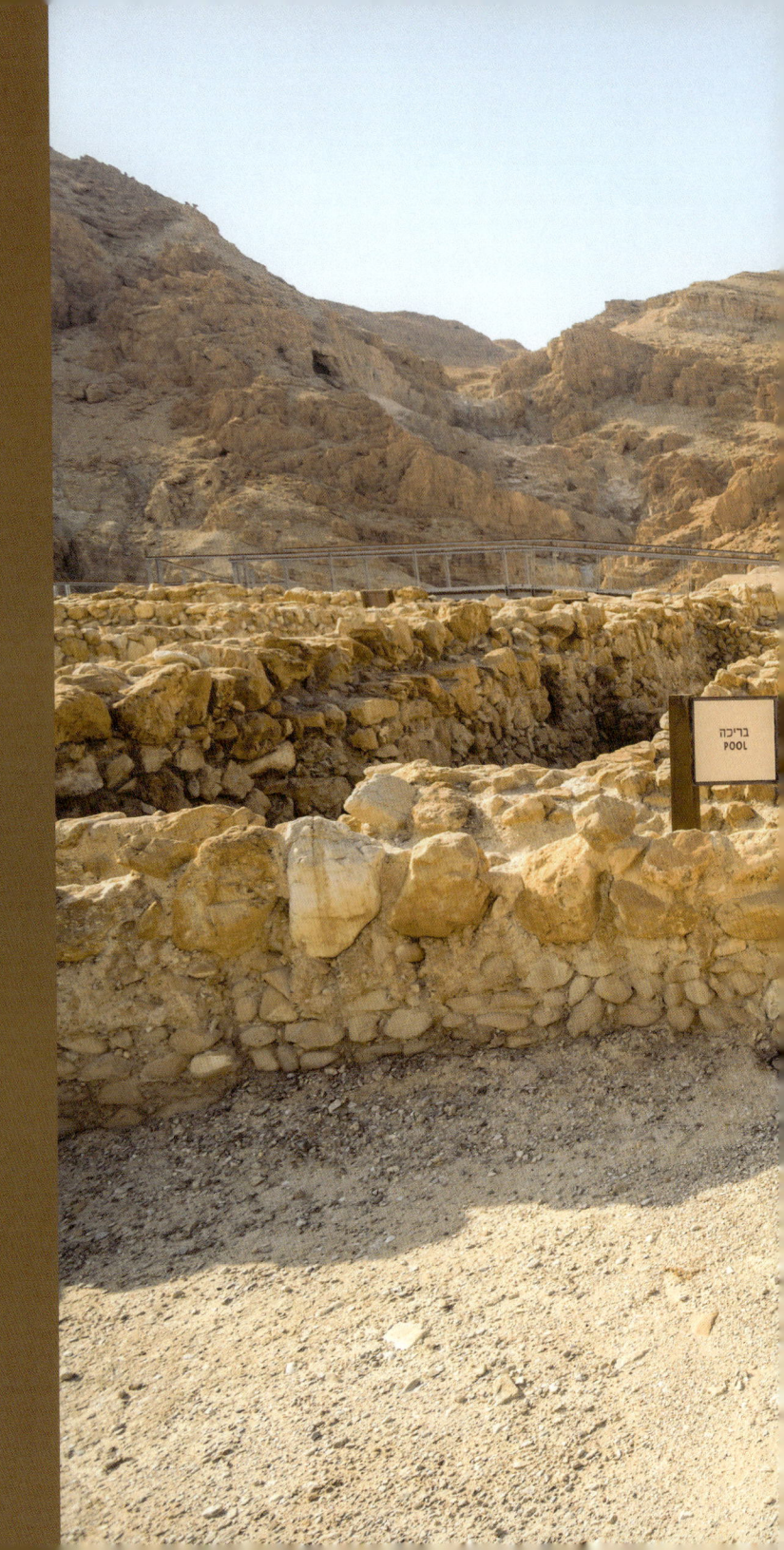

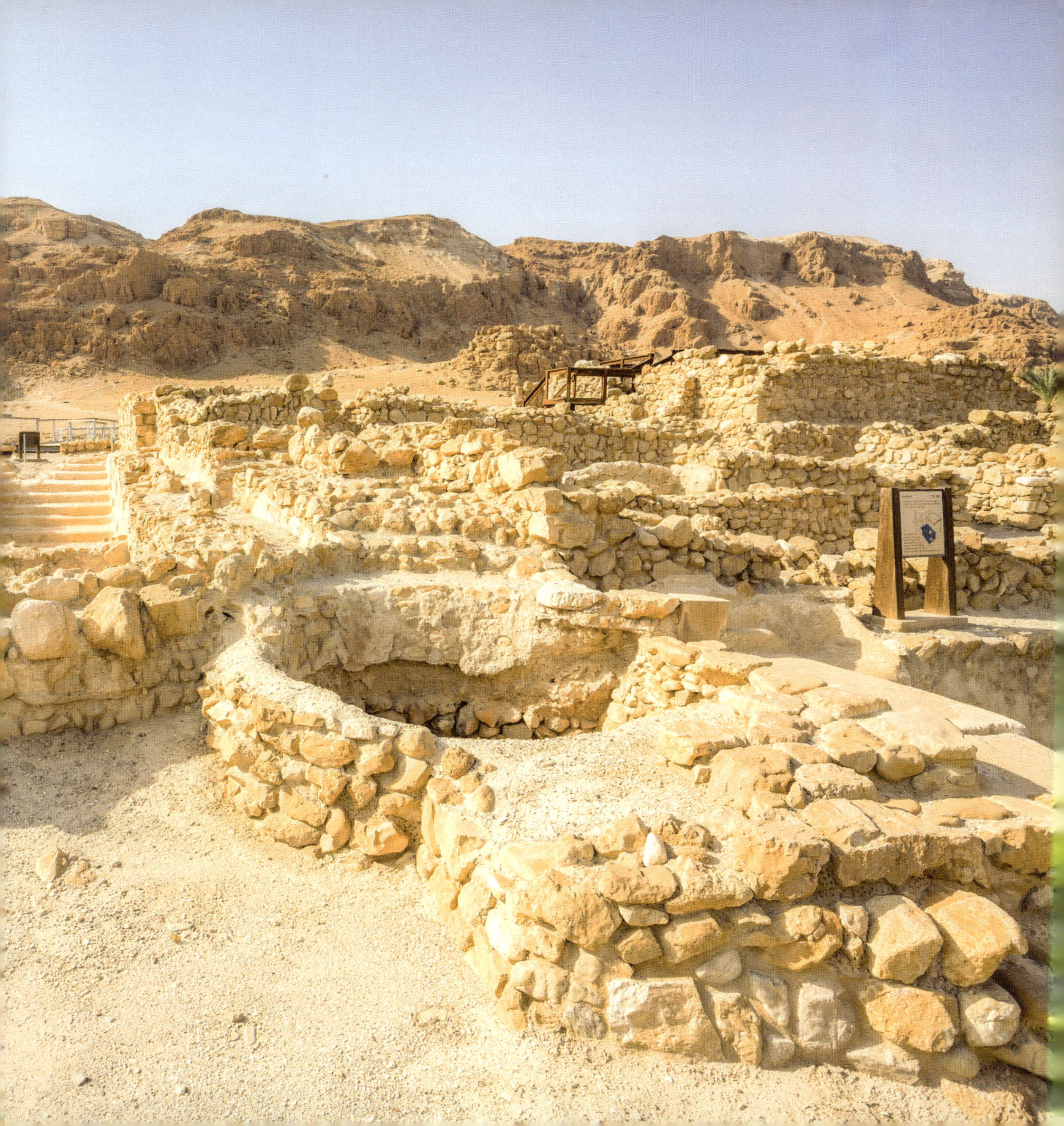

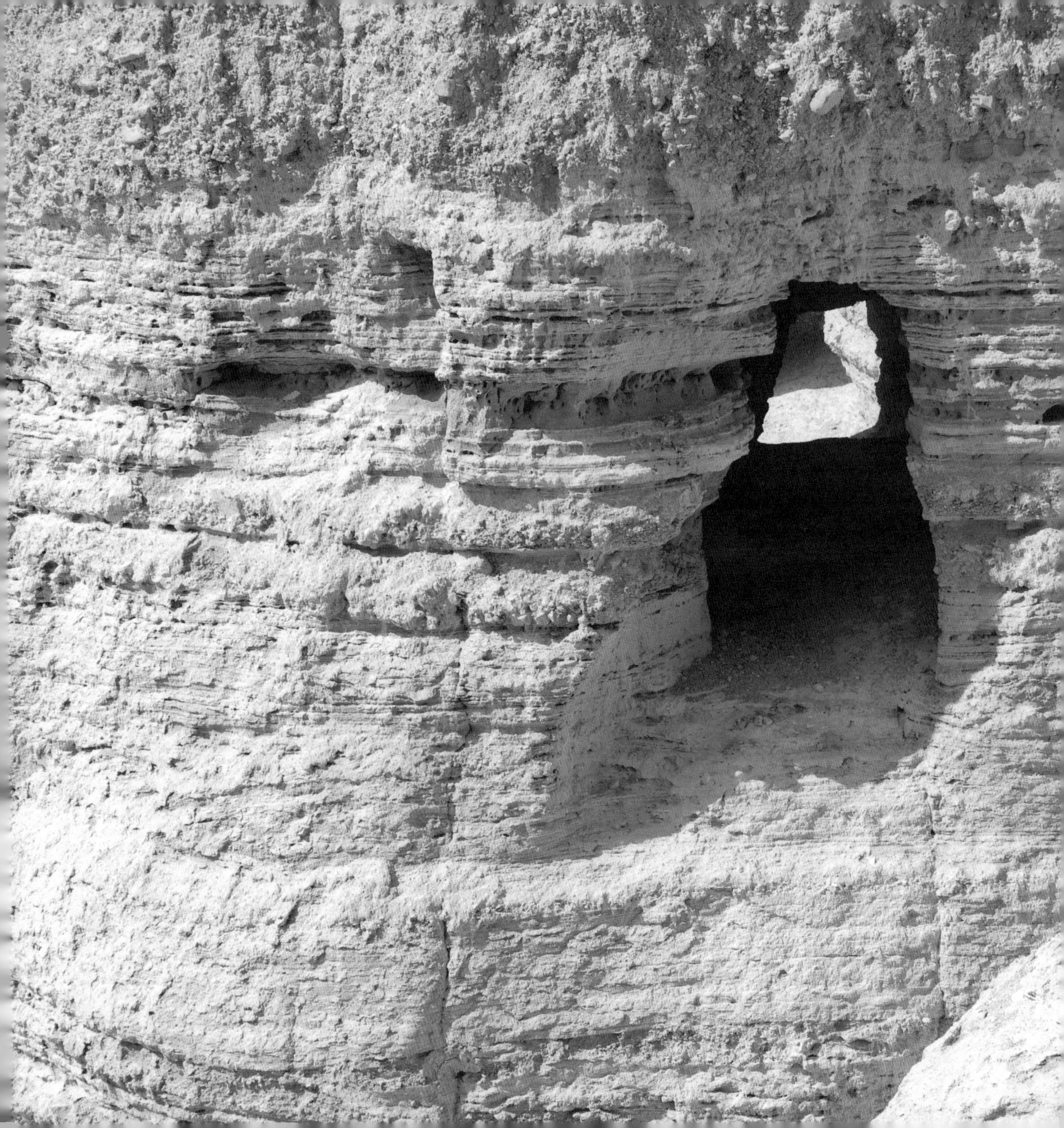

Most texts were written in Hebrew, some in Aramaic, and a few of the scripts were in Greek. The scrolls were traditionally identified with the ancient Jewish sector called Essenes.

Pompeii

Pompeii, an ancient Roman city, was literally erased from the map after Mount Vesuvius erupted in August 24, 79 AD.

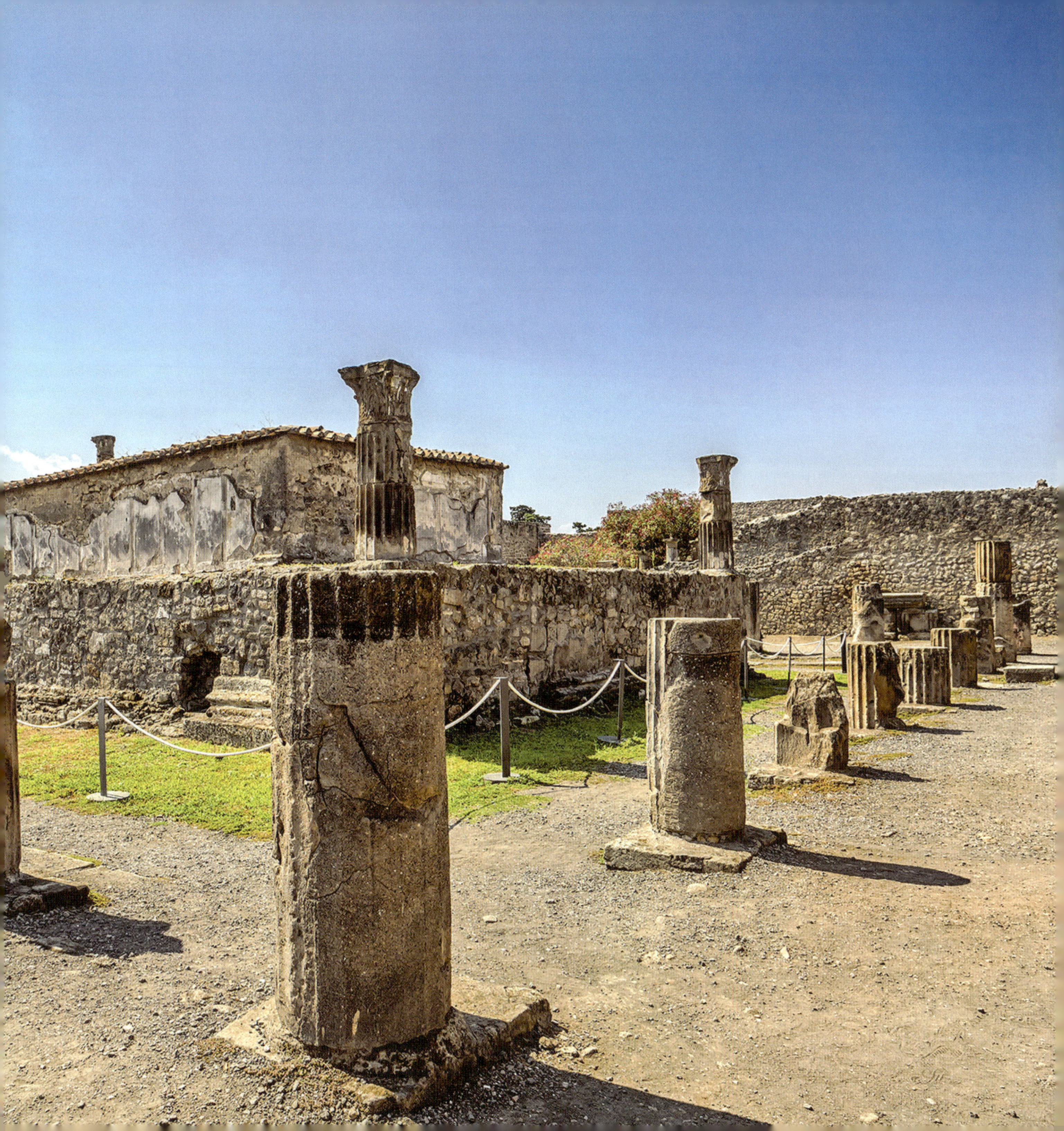

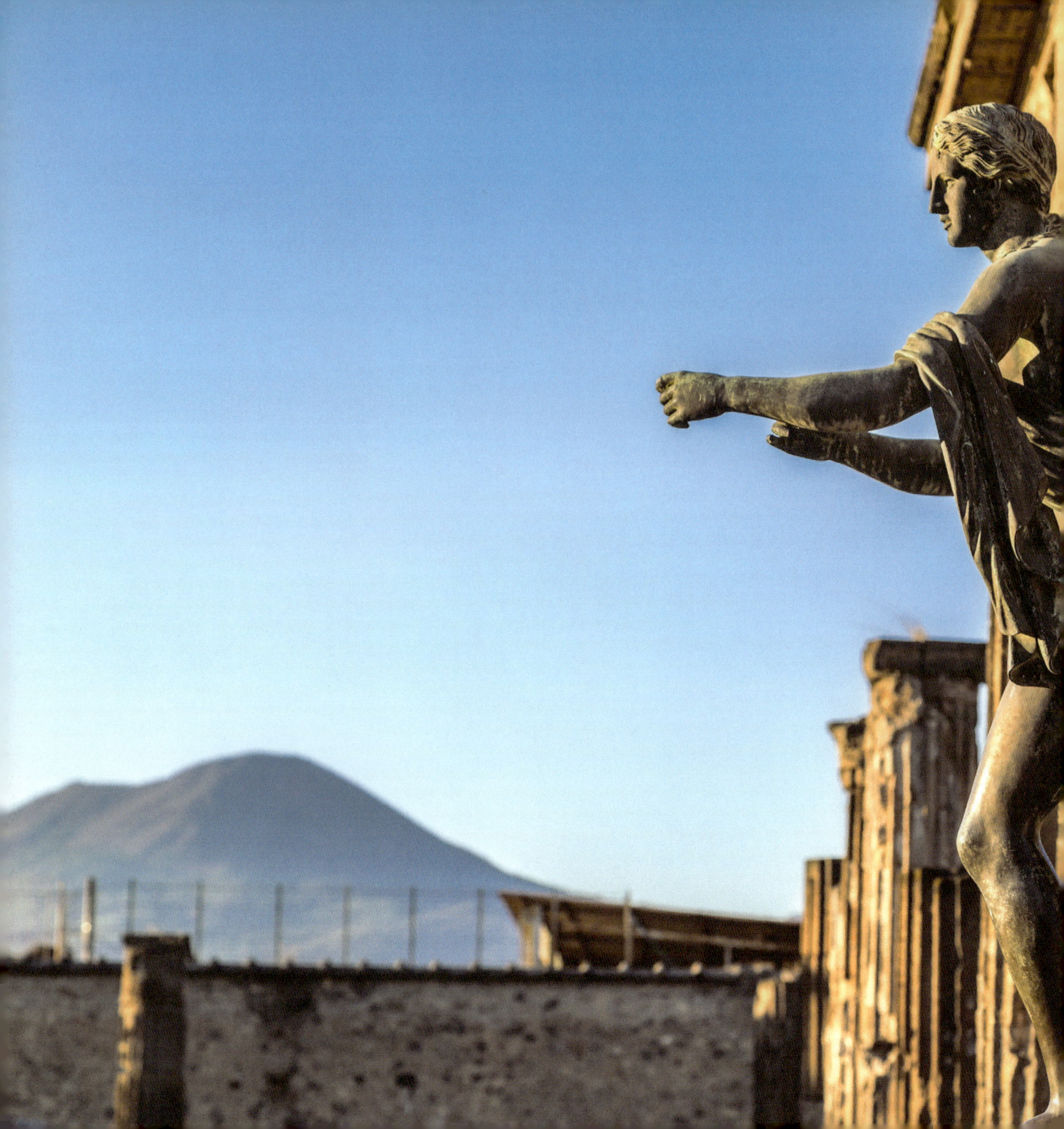

The volcano ejected the largest recorded debris clouds, twice the height of Mount Everest.

The City of Pompeii was covered with volcanic ashes that are 16 feet deep.

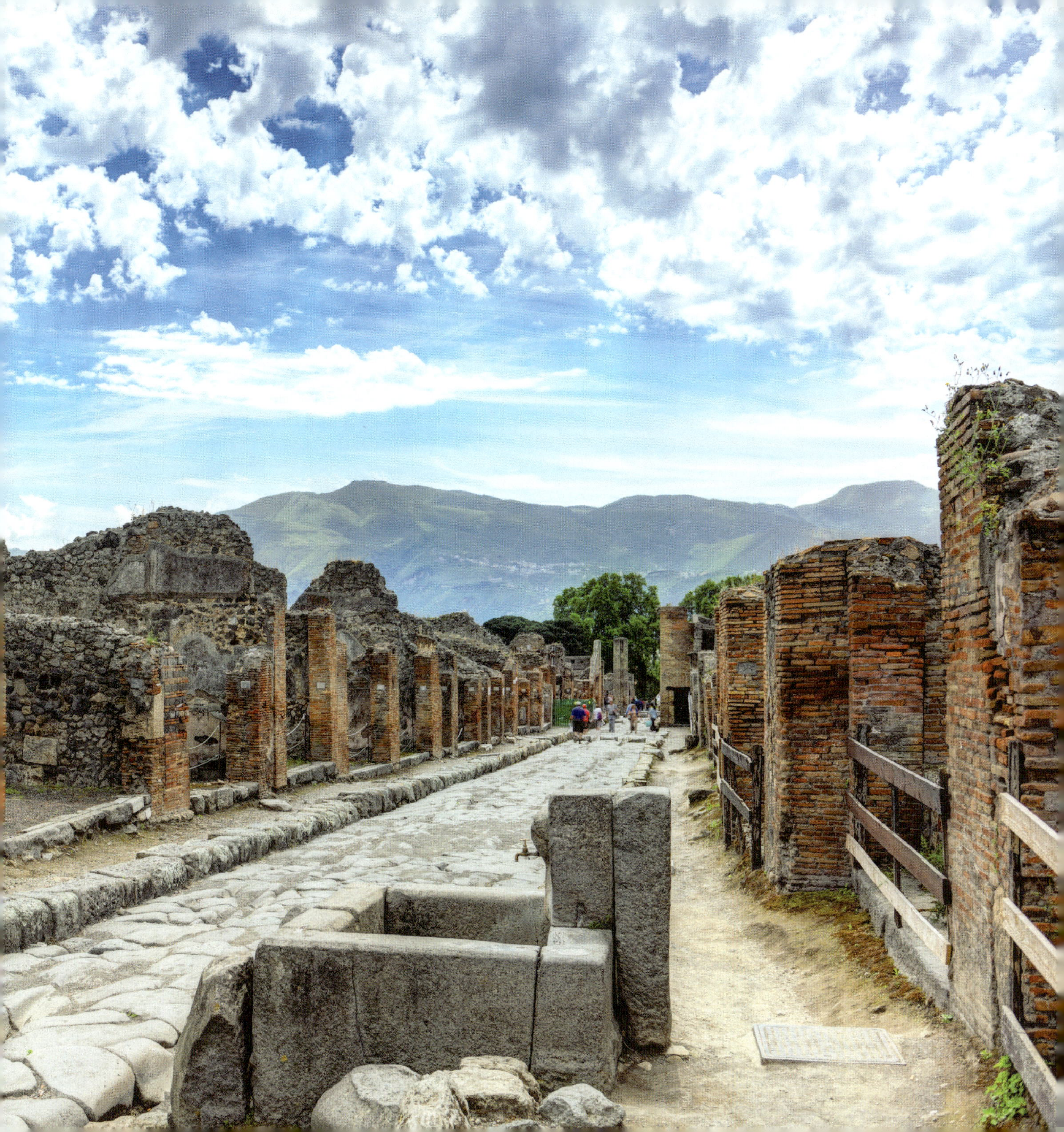

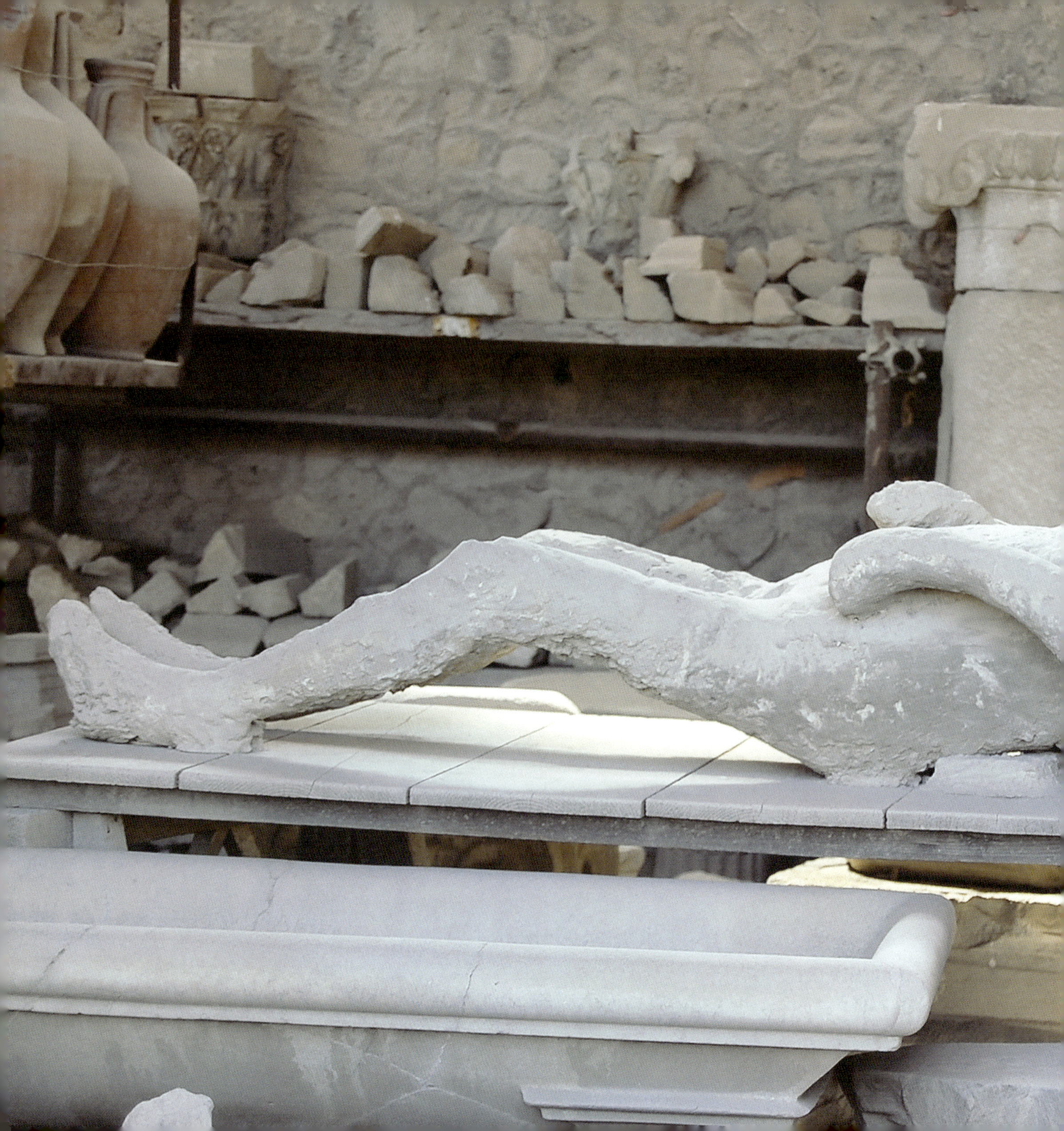

The ashes and pumice were very hot and they travelled very fast. With such powerful combination, they erased everything along their path.

Two thousand people died but were preserved in layers of volcanic debris so archaeologists were able to see them in their last moments.

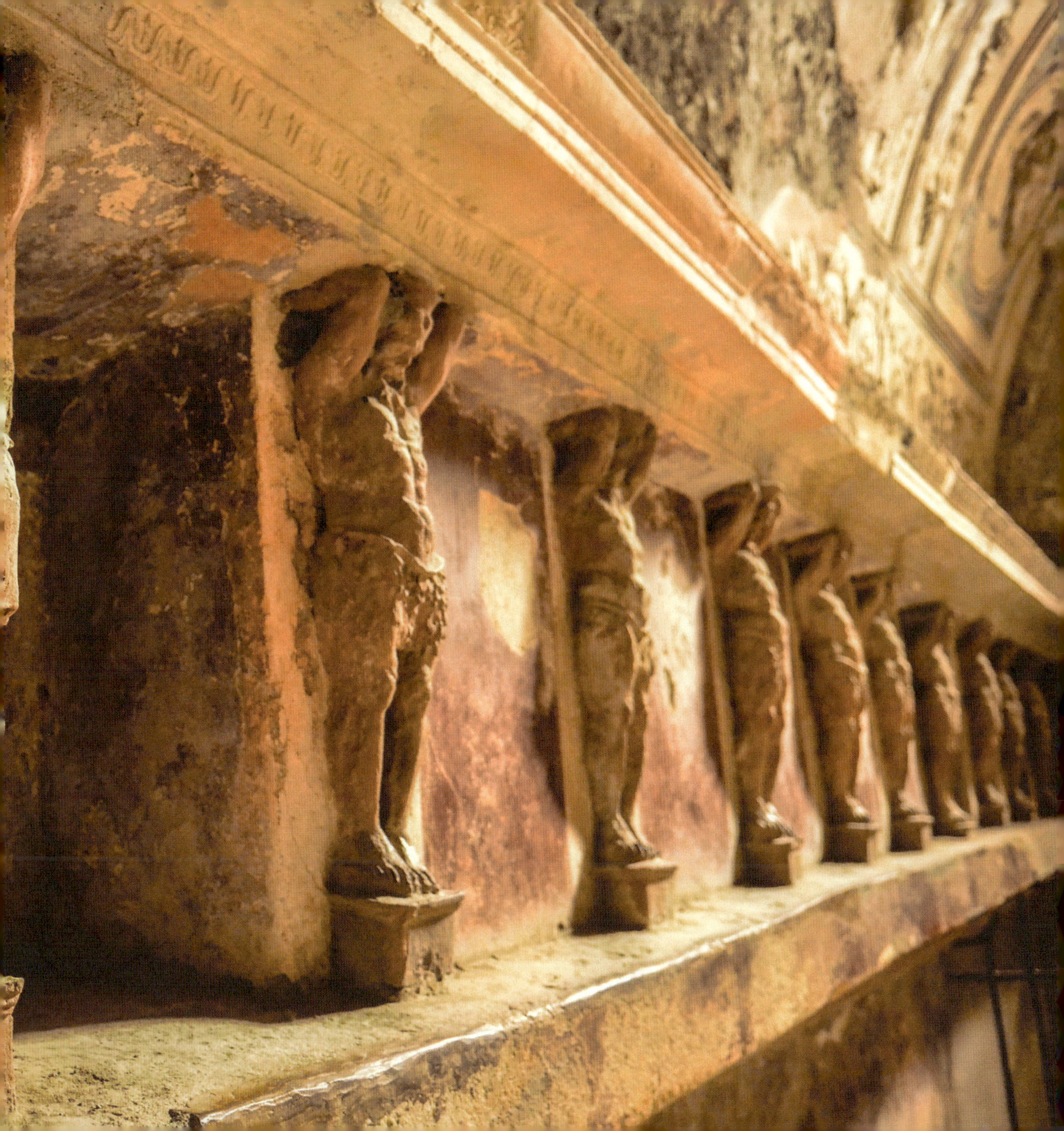

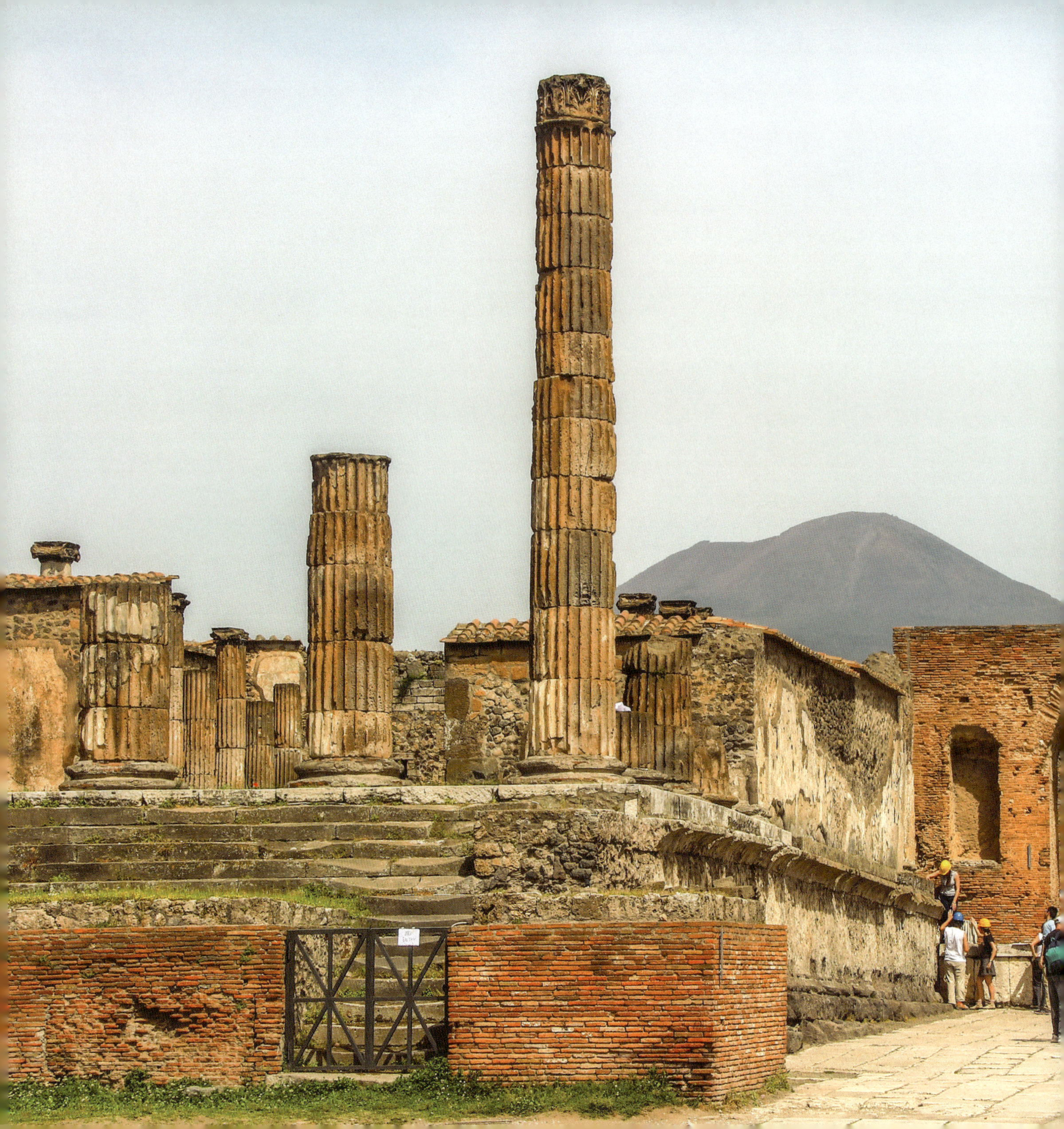

To this day, Pompeii is one of the most visited tourist attractions in Italy. About one third of the city is still buried even today.

Terracotta Army of Xi'an

The Terracotta Army of Xi'an is one of the greatest archaeological discoveries in the 20th century.

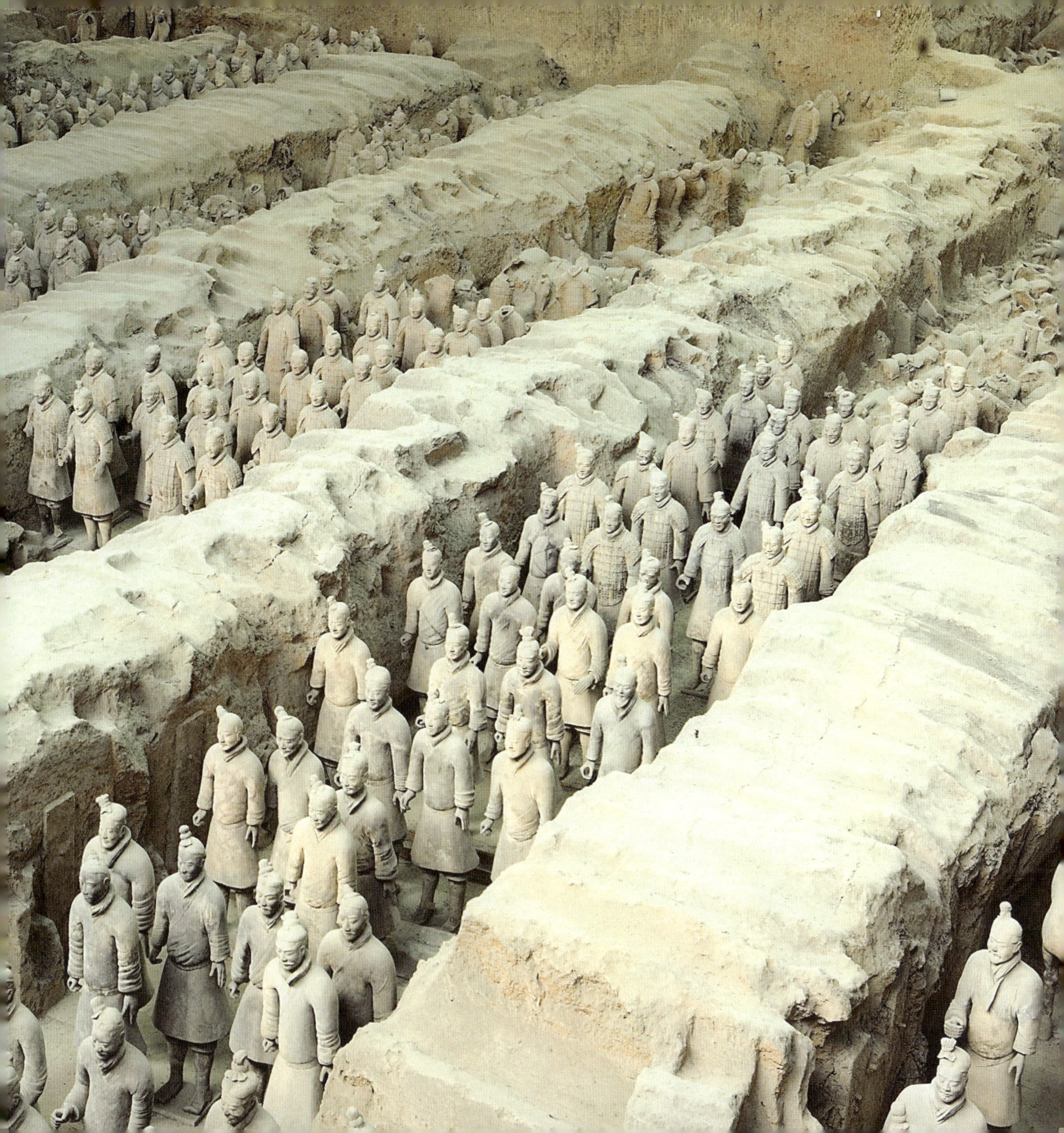

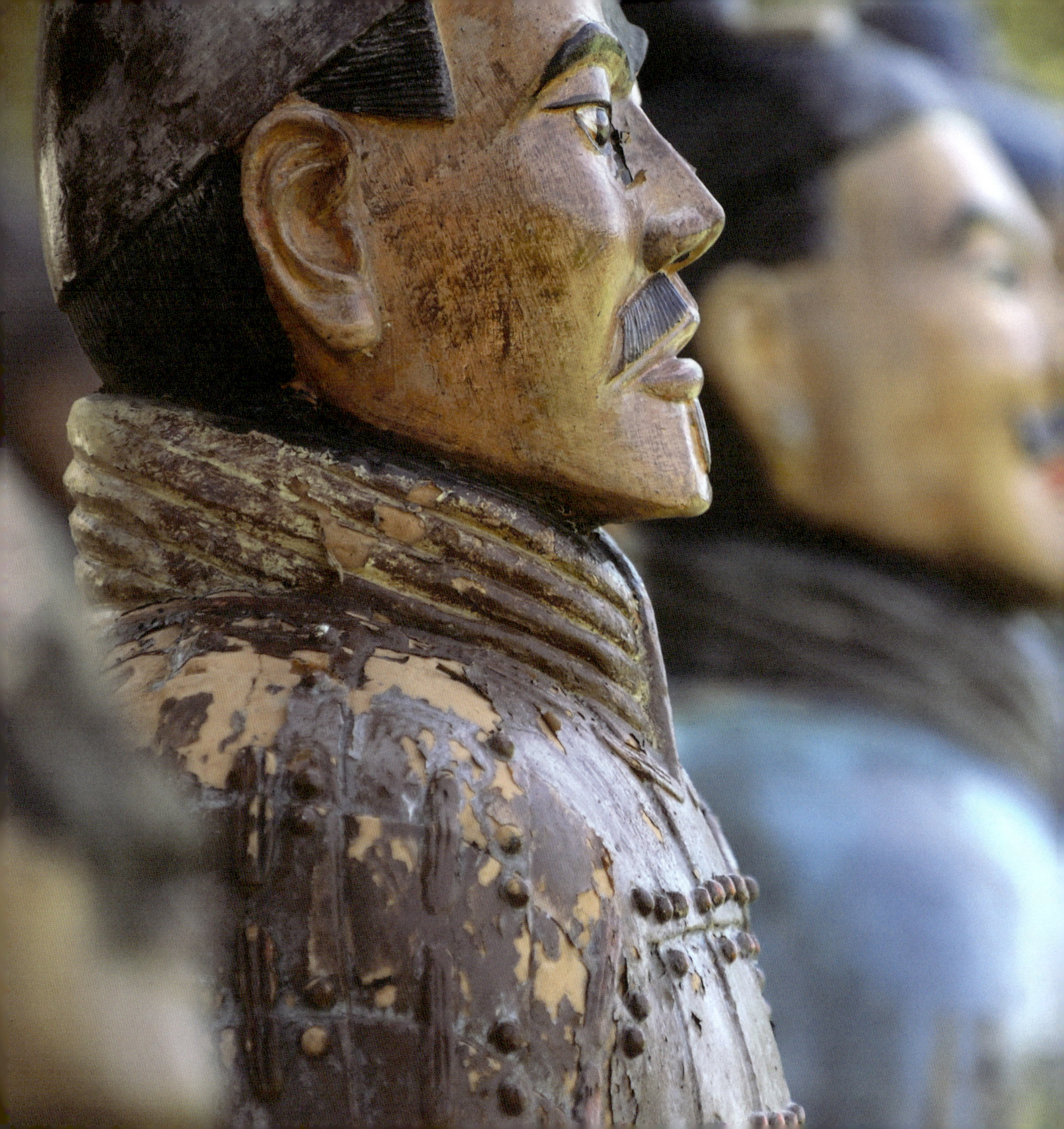

It is a display of hundreds of life-sized monuments of armies who triumphed over all Chinese armies during the period of Warring States before the imperial Chinese era in the last 2,200 years.

Archaeologists perform the very important job of finding valuale artifacts that show us what the past was like. What will they dig up next?

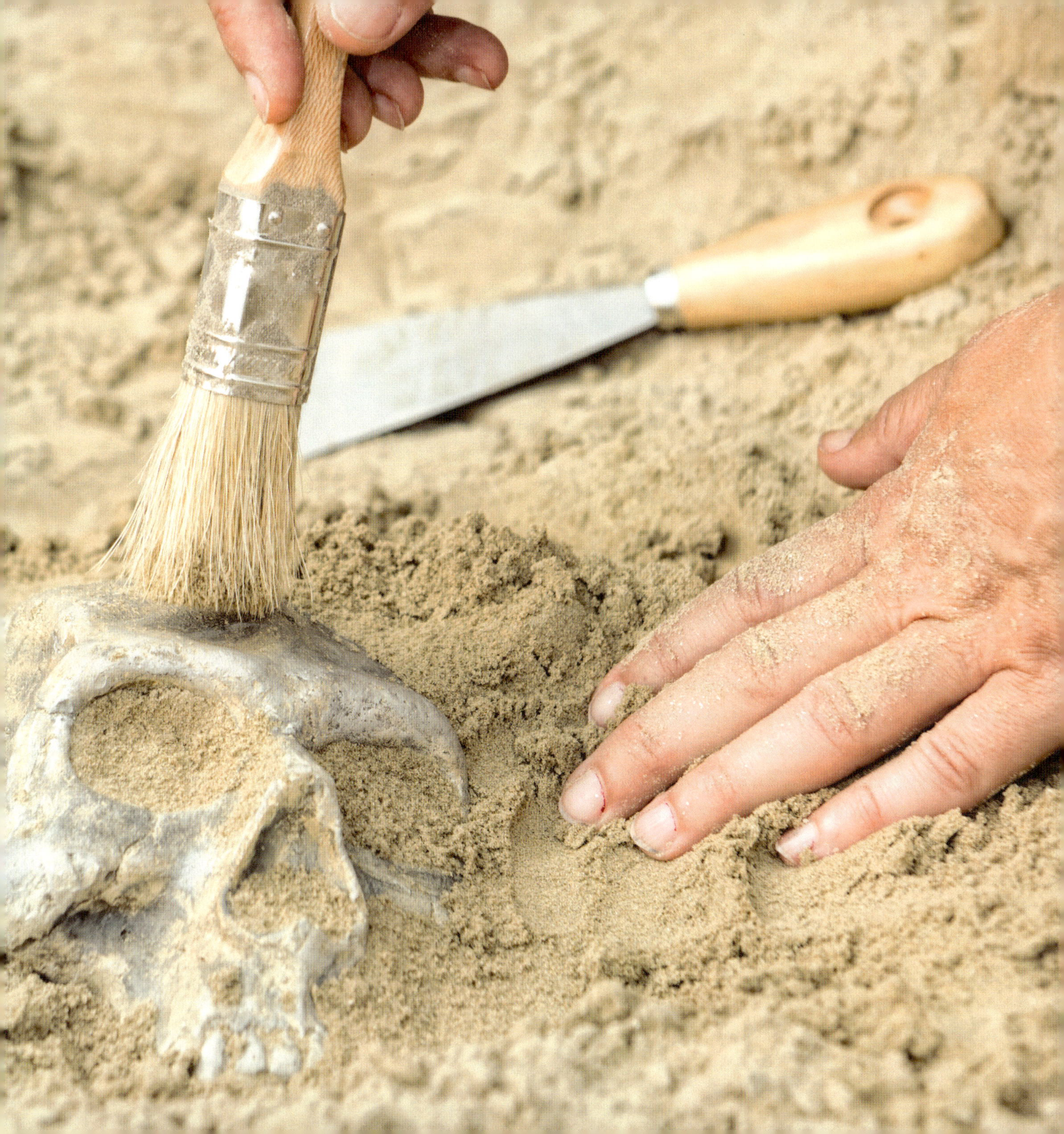

Printed in Great Britain
by Amazon